I CAN HEAR YOU BETTER WITH MY GLASSES ON!

Mildred M. Stokes

I CAN HEAR YOU BETTER WITH MY GLASSES ON!
Text Copyright © 2018 by Mildred M. Stokes

All rights reserved. No part of this book may be reproduced or transmitted in any form or by any means, electronic or mechanical, including photocopying, recording, or by any information storage and retrieval system, without written permission from the publisher. The only exception is brief quotations for reviews.

Cover Image by Business stock/Shutterstock.com

For information address:
J2B Publishing LLC
4251 Columbia Park Road
Pomfret, MD 20675

www.J2BLLC.com
GladToDoIt@gmail.com

Printed and bound in the United States of America.
This book is set in Minion Pro. Designed by Mary Barrows.

ISBN: 978-1-941927-74-8- Paperback
       978-1-941927-75-5- Hardback

I CAN HEAR YOU BETTER WITH MY GLASSES ON!

Mildred M. Stokes

Also by
Mildred M. Stokes

ROMANCING THE BEAUTIFUL DIVINE
A Joy Embrace Story Devotional

DEDICATION

This dedication is my thankfulness for the family of encouragers at Life Journeys Writers Guild and for its founder, our tireless leader, Yvonne Medley. And for all whom I met along the way who saw my passion, believing this day ... all who are now poised to witness the new birth here penned.

Table of Contents

    9   Introduction

Community of One

- 13 *Dwelling Places*
- 15 *When Neighbors Seek*
- 17 *Civility*
- 19 *What If That Actually Happened?*
- 21 *Left of Me*
- 23 *Rx Fix-It*
- 25 *Party Over*

Birthed To Be

- 43 *I Am*
- 45 *Something Within*
- 47 *Out of the Box*
- 49 *Inward Parts*
- 51 *What's Her Name?*
- 53 *Getting the Wish She Wanted*
- 55 *Dream Train Comin'*

Say It Some More

- 29 *Put 'Em On*
- 31 *Not Staying*
- 33 *Back It Up*
- 35 *Speak A Word*
- 37 *Too Much Going On!*
- 39 *When Promises Go Unkept*

Quintessential Grit

- 59 *Just Joy*
- 61 *Courage*
- 63 *Some More, Please!*
- 65 *The Other Pressure*
- 67 *Plantings In My Garden*
- 69 *Learned Lessons*

Why Not Rejoice?

- 73 *Rainbow Promise*
- 75 *Choose Ye This Day!*
- 77 *Cumbersome*
- 79 *Glue Stuff - When Things Fall Away*
- 81 *Equity*
- 83 *Very Belly Merry!*
- 85 *To the Fullest*
- 87 *In Celebration*

- 90 *Now It's Your Turn...*
- 107 *Contact Info*
- 109 *Meet the Author*

• INTRODUCTION •

This first book of poems is an exploration into the enchantment of writing poetry. Musings shared are intentioned in meaningful use of line and verse as I ventured out.

First, I wrote to entertain readers. I wanted you all to know more about me as writer while recalling quiet remembrances of your own encounters. And to exchange moments of amusement and reflection in ways perhaps unlike before.

Second, I wanted to encourage fellow poets and writers to *go after your dream!* You don't have to be anyone other than yourself. But what helps most is to believe that what you have to offer is unique, long sought after and valuable.

Lastly, I wrote to celebrate what was confirmed—once again—to me:

> *I can be what is for me to be when I am willing wholeheartedly to do the work to become it.*

Releasing self from the captivity of procrastination and hesitation is a tough thing to plow through for many of us at times. But there comes a moment in life when you refuse to be your own stumbling block any longer. And you break free. I did. So can you.

Commit to love what is good to love and embrace all that returns to reward you for your diligence. In that place you encourage others.

Treasures await you and your network of friends and love ones across these pages. May you be inspired to find your joy connection from the beginning to the end!

Community of One

DWELLING PLACES

My address has a street number, a distinct name all its own.
Things delivered like junk mail or bills to pay, never left alone.

This place often returned to gives comfort and shelter
A welcoming place, home, familiar like no other.

Nature's presence resides there too
With her mixture of off seasoned, four seasons
Performing their song and dance on cue.

They arrive to greet me beyond metered rhyme,
Catching me silently entranced from time to time.

My favorite has always been the newness of spring.
Laced with crisp blooms, accenting fragrances galore
Dew kisses sprinkled in early dawn, admired and adored.

We are designated workers in this vast matrix of time;
Fixed in spoken Creation and of grace Divine.

Bless this home, O Lord I pray,
Safe keep it—in Your hands—by night and by day.

Be it so...Be it so.

WHEN NEIGHBORS SEEK

I caught them again—just like before,
peeking through their window blinds,
wanting to know more.

Thought they went unnoticed
what my watchful eyes saw.

How long this cat and mouse game continued?
I could not readily recall; but chose instead convenience,
not really wanting to know at all.

Now, who's fooling who?
Enough, enough!

The moment has come.
Time now overdue to discover,
time to meet and greet one on one.

I speak, they listen; they speak, I learn.

We pledge as helping neighbors
when shared needs come our way,
to encourage one another,
anchor strong and in so doing, stay.

The ice is now broken, unsure glances no longer stare.
No longer strangers spoken about in my prayers.

Now my chat flows freely, whether coming in or leaving out.
"How may I serve you, Neighbor?
Just give me a shout!"

CIVILITY

The word itself has a delicate ring,
encircles awareness, draws you in—
one that escorts you to attention.

Inherent tranquility is its destination,
each citizen obliged in consideration
one day at a time as we go.

This ideal charge to keep, unlegislated I am told;
rather a fountain flow of constant care for life,
a genuine respect for the soul.

One may ask curiously the extent of its reward;
Simply—balance, community and peace restored.

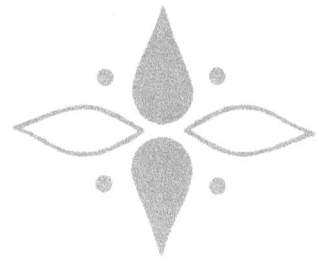

WHAT IF THAT ACTUALLY HAPPENED?

People of the world wait.
People of the world are waiting.

We are the world, never intended
just a song…sung to the rhythm of
the night…finger poppin'

Hands clappin' too…making
everything look like on stage,
dance crazed…*and all right!*

Everybody rockin' doing the rhythm.
Reality shows up…eyes opened…
when uncertainty checks in.

Are we truly ONE yet? *Or just on stage.*

                                          … still waiting …

LEFT OF ME

Out of all the all I've given,
you still want the more.

And what gets left behind?

Far too little of once I knew as me before,
...stripped down, unidentified!

Rx FIX-IT

A heaping dose of full belly laughter
is the medicine happenstance
gave to me—before and after.

Laughter resounded across both hemispheres
giggling wildly, staggering off balance a bit,
still kept in a gleeful fit.

All around me bands of merry hearts
gulped away lavish potions of this
elixir, Rx FIX-IT!

Laughter—drink it in, let it out;
good for the soul, warmth for the heart.

PARTY OVER

Know when *your* party is over.
No matter about the bass or
how loud the music plays.
Abandoned inhibitions rising like crazy
The pace more daringly unveiled.

Know when *your* party is over.
No matter about the bass. Consider the
change of scenery—pleasure offers on the exchange.

Listening, discernment quietly whispers, stirring up
within your core this now solemn notice, 'Hit the door!'

Time to excuse yourself,
gracefully take your leave.
Set your GPS for homeward bound
where safety greets well-pleased.
Adieu, party people, Adieu!

Unplugged.

Say It Some More

PUT 'EM ON

I can hear you better with my glasses on!
Have you heard this before and found it true?
The first time you put yours on you
discovered a whole new look about you!

They look funny on me—better on display, on that girl in red.
Better on him, dressed handsomely, shoes spit-shined,
His brim tilted just so and his countenance, all aglow!
They sure know how to put 'em on.

I can hear you better with my glasses on!
My mom and dad, my auntie's cherished quilt club—
even my neighbor next door, all say it. *All the time!*
Kinda' unsettles me a bit sitting here in my reclina'.

Shucks! I'm puttin' my glasses on—
just to see who's right or who's wrong.
See?

NOT STAYING

Staying stuck down is to choose accepting accommodated excuses.
With great desire, decide Not Staying! Climbing out unleashes a
bold paradigm shift towards victory—a story not to be hidden from view,
But shared. Someone's waiting for hope's guidance, out there.

Blaming—invades truth, embitters the soul—rehearsing widely
deepened offences. When fixed on staying stuck down, now convinced
in error. Giving into *nothing else left to do.*

A convenience, befitting for seekers in search of an ideal escape.
An easy out, no responsibility, no part played—so claimed.
I'm innocent, told to self, *a case of life preyed upon me, believed.*

No, not staying…
Not staying stuck down in despair.
My journey story's unwrapped, it must be shared.
Someone's waiting for hope's guidance, out there.

BACK IT UP

Anyone will grab hold to almost
anything thrown out to rescue them.
Careful! *Desperation will do you like that.*

Weariness tries to fix your stare on doom
when your breakthrough is on its way—actually quite soon.

Hold on! *Ride out the storm!*

Unlike then, you well-know now what you didn't know before.
The source and strength of your life is Him, in Jesus Christ the Lord.

Adjust your focus and set your direction,
No longer bound, armed with protection.

SPEAK A WORD

Like the 'Sisters', I stand declaring.
Under no wavering circumstances
I choose to say what needs to be said
right now!

Time is the occasion of chaos breaking out
in diverse places.
Let there be peace.

Time is missed when foolish things
unseat weightier matters.
Let there be desire for peace.

Time is when texting becomes the dominant norm,
preferred over face to face presence.
Let there be peace between us.

Time is when our lives are such busy places
I miss you, you the same; yet we don't even know why.
Let there be found peace among us all.

TOO MUCH GOING ON!

Up 'fore day in the morning.
High noon has come
No breakfast for me done
Too much going on.

Bell ringing at the front door
Dog scratching at the back
Kids hair pullin', elbowing,
Pushing, shoving at the mirror
I call out, but they won't stop.

Is it a sibling rivalry going on?
Or some vengeance not talked about?

*"Stop barking, McKenzie …
Wait your turn!"*

Gotta solve more pressing concerns
Like bringing folk to the table
To hash things out–as best I am able.

Reconciled to forgive,
Reconciled to let bygones
Be bygone!

*"Doggone McKenzie,
interrupting me again—
come in. Come on in…"*

Too much going on!

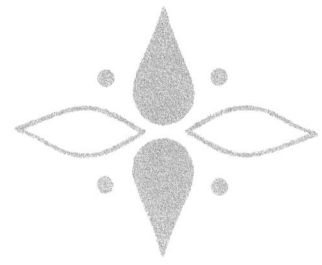

WHEN PROMISES GO UNKEPT

Good news surprises?
A gleeful smile, a calm assurance;
something marvelously intended.

Good news promises?
Sends the heart beating anxiously;
overflowing this time in great expectations!

But those promises that go unkept,
especially in the most unlikely of situations—

Can be disastrous!
　　　　　When was your last—one?

Birthed To Be

I AM

I am from a noble past, my mother and father—
and all theirs, before them.

I am from some place before nature's harmonies,
the past present—the beginning.

I am from the Omnipotent, Omnipresent, and Omniscient One—
He who loved me long before my presence
was coined by someone else's
imagination or passion borne.

I am from He who ushers and preserves me
across every destined tomorrow.
Yes, I am here.
I belong!

SOMETHING WITHIN

Like the seasons, there is a time
For the birth of newness, the shedding of what was
So that something valuable, secretly hidden from view
no longer wrestles tirelessly to be free. There is such a time.

If the one held captive should know the exact moment,
Would that one hasten towards the offering of peace?
Or would we hear squeaking and squawking,
"Not yet, not now, not me!"

(Clinging to yesterday, going nowhere faster and faster.)

So then, when is this time?
This ideal place or space—the right season
To burst forth strong and joyously—fragrant
In the embrace of The Beautiful Divine.

In the fullness of time,
Answer the call.

[Reprinted from: Mildred M. Stokes, Romancing the Beautiful Divine, A Joy Embrace Story Devotional. c.2014. Outskirts Press. ISBN: 978-1-4787-0052-4.]

OUT OF THE BOX

Fears, released away
along with everything else
let go from you.
Fear—disembodied, powerless.

No longer compromised with the
paralysis of accompanying discontent,
disapprovals of missteps made,
unforgiven seemingly, without delay.

Love not there before, now is
embraced in all its splendor!

Private spaces, heretofore reserved
sacred for fear to rule, no longer hold
you—boxed in.

INWARD PARTS

Born into a fallen world
fashioned in my mother's womb.
Yet *'fearfully wonderful!'*
This essence I am.

Your eyes, O God, saw my substance true;
those inward parts skillfully sorted through,
fused into formation: lungs, belly, heart,
sinew—just to name a select few.

Nurtured all the while
in the shelter of her love.
Concealed in the folds of her daily life lived,
my gestation was framed—ordained.

Given that one chance,
I came, and brought relief.
Birthed that day through required pain,
in hope—then joy released.

Yes, You knew me well
in that womb place long before the first wail
or the first blessed sight to see.

You embraced me, O God
and spoke: *"Come forth, let her be.*
For my image bearer has arrived—this mystery!"

WHAT'S HER NAME?

Something has been told, broadcast to the village.
All who hear celebrate, now believing:
The miracle has been birthed. I am set free!

Then comes the chatter, the question of the day,
Begging to be asked and dissected in every away.
What's her name?

Does it speak of the past, if not this present?
Or is it an oracle of what is to come?
To remind us, the Master's will shall be done.

Does it call out to the ancestors?
Do elders need to rehearse
village birthing songs, so many now forgotten…

Does her name rejoice in the voice of
the sun and all the star lit nights shone,
far away—in the mother kingdom?

Perhaps, just maybe.

And with this miracle arrival shall it bring healing to our lands?
So that joy takes on life's center stage, guided towards purposed plan.

How may we find out? How can we be sure?

Now, now… cease worry, since it is His time alone who knows.
Divine manifestations have already been decided
And so it is—forevermore.

GETTING THE WISH SHE WANTED

It started when she was past a tot
knowing little about wanting
what she should want not.

Gretchen wanted her own bed to sleep in
not having to share seemingly ad infinitum,
with one of her many oversized siblings.

Living large meant just what it said,
in a relatively small dwelling, limiting space
which Gretchen always felt cramped in,
with no place to go, no place for escape.

This day an ottoman became her sleep nest.
Oh, how she loved having her own!
A prized possession to hold her in place,
Gretchen imagined herself exalted —

A QUEEN seated high on her ottoman throne.

DREAM TRAIN COMIN'

Now that the day has done
all that any day can do,
I lay me down to rest.

Trickles of moon light
stealing through window frame cracks,
chase after LED streams, peeking
from my morning alarm, android screen.

In unison, both forcing me to turn over
and hurry—not a second to lose.
Gotta' catch that dream sleep groove.

Quintessential Grit

JUST JOY

JOY, promised to come this morning after a disquieting uncertainty.
It was those moments when all that was left to do was to do absolutely nothing.
And yet my despair persisted—tugging away incessantly.

Now it happened when restfulness crept in disguised,
after countless nights of sheep counting anxiously abided.
Covers of sleep's warmth embraced my bare bone shoulders;
as I felt surrender, snuggling in gently all at once—all over.

I sensed my purring, almost like that of a cat's, I first thought.
Only mine trumpeted through the barren sound of hush across the room.
Mine, across those many spent nights, abandoned to myself—consumed.

At last! Ever so calmly, the breaking of dawn brushed against my brow
Awakening me with the hope of gladness, prayed for
again and again before. It whispered in graceful authority—

Good Morning, JOY!

COURAGE

What is it? I mused.
Could it possibly be *so* simple,
In everything … always?
What, if it answered, Yes? What, if, No?
In every situation
Whether great or small,
This hope thing called
Courage is … real.
Oh, so very real …

Live in it!

SOME MORE, PLEASE!

Courage takes on a certain boldness to go it alone
if you have to—and even when you don't want to.
Because it matters.

Courage pursues the knowledge of truth
where the stakes are sky high and so much gets lost
forever, so little gained—without mindful pursuit.

Courage takes strength, all elements thereof,
the physical, emotional, the spiritual—even financial.
Invested currency advances the mission truth deposits to the light.

Run, go hide, pretend an invincible self should you dare.
But as for me, I'll stand. Life is the vision conceived,
not lasting long to see. Dare not chance it,
nor bet against its opportunity!

Casting away hidden fears, the doubting stares of naysayers
And stinging jeers from envy-hearted scoffers, I take leave.
I cry out, *"More courage, O God, please!"*

THE OTHER PRESSURE

There is this pressure we know about;
It's the one we often deny,
When we obsess with
Having things our way.
We leave no room to oblige.

We miss the chance
Any needing person might earnestly desire
To be considered, heard, even prayed over,
Loved, embraced and inspired.

What if right then and there
You took off *your* mask
And allowed truth to prevail.
Exposed your own vulnerabilities,
Your anxieties, your fears and oft recurring despair.

Publicly showing seated front row in pew,
how desperately your heart hungers too—
for recognition, a safe place,
for the freedom to simply
be *You*.

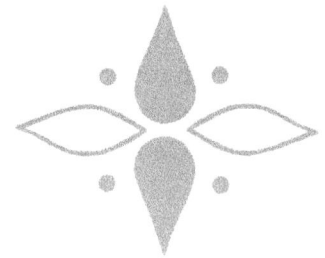

PLANTINGS IN MY GARDEN

Why do we quarrel over simple things?
Why do we open sores and contend?
Although it is hardly imaginable our world
in the absence of such underpins.

Yet because we have been given much on our plate
Direct from the Master's love, there remains
the path to heal our minds and touch
our hearts with grace—

How so then?

The spirit of love, of power and strong seeds planted with sound mind too. The solution appointed, under His anointing, now our faltering hearts beat with this truth.

For it is how our Provider, the Master Gardener, has set this correction irrevocably, this which He orchestrated:

That we befriend one another as a global community, and not disdain inherent diversities we are bound to, hiding behind impunity and greed in our hearts while the world waits once again, tarnished.

The sprinkling of effectual affection, sustenance set in place to sustain us, persists beyond the abyss of any selfish discomfort displayed towards unalike others.

Therefore love. This unclaimed gift remaining sits—a challenge to the nations—as each one tills unapologetically, the soil of their resistance.

LEARNED LESSONS

... it isn't always easy to feel forgiven
perched from your lofty view.
Most times it's about first forgiving yourself
which tends to be hardest of the two.

● ● ●

... it's best not to compare yourself to others' best,
nor covet what's assigned as theirs.
Sure, be inspired!
be totally committed to the best
self can do.
You'll find it more than enough for you!

● ● ●

... indeed, two people can look at the exact same thing
and see something totally different.
My perspective versus yours, both
judging what we say that we saw.

Freeze! Each of us can be right— on pause.

Why Not Rejoice?

RAINBOW PROMISE

Touch with your heart the ribbon of hues,
in draped innocence across the sky—

after the rain waters the dust and saturates the fields,
causing the brooks to babble so alive.

Then you would know a single act of the Creator's love,
His covenant, a promise—seedtime and harvest given.

This rainbow sign, a reminder extended—from the Heart
Who reigns from above.

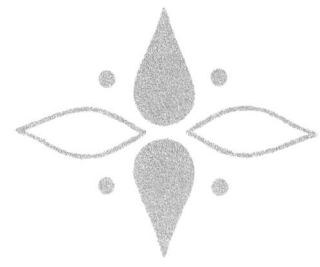

CHOOSE YE THIS DAY!

Back in the day you had choices when you went to the egg market.
Pullets, small, large, extra large and jumbo were the egg sizes I recall.
Nowadays most store clerks don't have a clue.
If you're not buying large—it's easy.

Select extra large and keep it movin'.

Recipes are simplified too: egg size doesn't matter anymore, at all.
Just crack an egg, let it splatter, cook, plate and serve.

Now the exception is the chicken! Grass fed, cage free, organic or not.
Prices, packaging and egg color clearly indicate what you've got.

So when the Pastor reads *"Choose Ye this day Whom you will serve."*
Only two options are God-given: Life or Death. How simple was that!?

The tough part is our tendency to wander, having selected one over the other. Our imperfection is primal.

Our obsession with unreasonable wants gets in the way. Plan A versus Plan B sounds simple enough—

> I mean easier said,
> then soon,
> undone!

CUMBERSOME

The more cumbersome, the recall itself recoils more around everything.
The trauma of bad touch in its truest forms—reminding still.
Now daily healing through the sieve of tenderness, and release.

> Layer by layer,
> Scrub through—all
> the way back.

All the way to those wonderment years, expecting as any child would,
To be cared for and protected from those corrupt ones who cared not at all
concerning an innocent's potential—their present and destined tomorrows.

> Misused, abused moments in time
> This way and that,
> Remembered.
> still aching…

> *Yet, I shall live on.*

GLUE STUFF - WHEN THINGS FALL AWAY

Humpty Dumpty was in deep trouble,
So goes humanity.

Humpty Dumpty had a really, big fall,
So did humanity.

Humpty Dumpty could not be pieced together,
Not so humanity.

The glue-stuff we're privy to patches us up unlike any other.
The turbulent tides we're caught up in, called s-i-n
Contends with the Holy Spirit who engages to defend.

What is this miracle concoction, you may ask of me?
Redemption through the Risen Lord, free to all who believe.

To know Creator God still loves me—imperfections and all
Is a mind-blowing proposition, indeed!

The greater significance is not what I did when, nor didn't do even then. But rather the matter is what He did unconditionally for me…

He put me back together again!

EQUITY

I spied their willingness to stay.
Their deeply-etched resolve to stand
against all that stands in the way.

Equity women, not taking it any more!
Not going back, diminished by the rhetoric of politics.
Stooped by fear of not being believed
when the winds of raw truth are revealed.

Resigned to stay the course at the
urgency of the hour.
You and me, me too and you,
the strength of willpower strong.

This time stayed, in drum beat rhythm
until all our victories, united
ARE ONE!

VERY *BELLY* MERRY!

Journey pilgrims we are, seeking life's pleasure moments—
basking in the joy of glad tidings' presence.
Yet finding woes strewn along the path as we run.

The good news of comfort speaks: "Trouble don't last always!"

Last time laughed, laughter brought more laughs than before.
Last time laughed, laughter brought sighs and tears of relief.

Laughter, the sound that caresses the heavens with gladness.
The sound, that thanks the earth for giving us so much;
Gifting comfort, friendship and a steady hand up.

No matter what key or stanza you come in on,
hiccups in life creep in unannounced, unwanted
always some greater than before—while others remain small.

A prayer, a meditation, strained moments waiting amused,
might be all you'll have to carry you all the way through.

So then, when was the last time
you belly-laughed
out loud?

TO THE FULLEST

The last thing she invited me to do
is the first thing that sent my mind racing,

"Go live your life!" is what she spoke
so gently laced in earnest hope.

Stored away dreams some time ago created
Unearthed echoes of starry-eyed promises outdated
Beckoned me to *un-bucket list* those treasured goals.

For heaven's sake,
Get on with it…

"Go live your life, too!"

IN CELEBRATION

Those who decide, "I shall live—even if I must die!"
We read about them, even pray for their lineage,
those who germinate out of their brave-borne stories.

We celebrate the height of their historic sojourn, the heroes--these
courageous women and men defending our freedom from shore to shore.

For those fallen or wounded in ruinous battles we raise up a banner of
honor, a salute, a deep gratitude to every one of you.

And to your families who sacrificed alongside believing, a very special
warm thanks to each of you too!

Now remains with us, many a humble decorated soldier;
representing the battle-wearied souls across time.

The fate of humanity hangs in the balance, it's true.
Our carbon footprints will give us away; we shall be found.

That said:
There will be no hiding places at roll call,
on that great and dreadful Day in the skies.

But still we rejoice and we move. We have our being and strength in
celebration of hope, courage and love.

>   In faith's wisdom,
>   this is our desire.

NOW, IT'S YOUR TURN...

These next pages are left open for you to begin your musings.
There exists no better time like this present to declare your say.
Write to delight yourself, digging in and down under for the gems placed within.
Dance. Even sing, if you must; evoke silence and earth to temper things down.
Imagine and let your heart-thoughts fly freely.
However steep the summit climb, embrace its vastness of possibility.
And there receive, in fullness of health, all that is named to you.
Pursue!

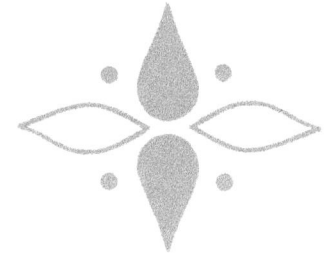

Feel invited to engage me:

Book & Poetry Club Meet-Ups

Conferences, seminars & sales incentives

Customized Poetry Creations

'Get Living' Group & Solo Consults

Intermission Entertainment

Spoken Word Stage Press

Wellness Mining & How It Heals

Writing Your Way to Finding Optimal Health

Contact Info:

Mildred...Speaking!

Bus. Ofc. 301-336-0151

Mobile: 301-751-0765

Email: reach4health@gmail.com

Meet the Author

Mildred M. Stokes

No stranger to writing, Stokes' first book, *Romancing the Beautiful Divine*, is a story devotional that includes meditation challenges and a prayer blessing at the end of each chapter. Stokes is a retired educator and is currently the Director of the Health and Wellness Ministry at Calvary Gospel Church in Waldorf, MD.

As Certified Fitness Nutrition Specialist and health promoter, Stokes' passion to advance nutritional health and complete wellness in communities is underway.

"Writing has been a regular part of my work life journey," she says, "and creative poetry accompanies me along the continuum of health to wealth advocacy, informative writing, public speaking and joyful encouragement."

www.ingramcontent.com/pod-product-compliance
Lightning Source LLC
Chambersburg PA
CBHW071148090426

42736CB00012B/2272